A JOY-SPARKING ILLUSTRATED JOURNEY
THROUGH THE FIRST **60** LESSONS OF
A COURSE IN MIRACLES WORKBOOK

Dedicated to your next miracle!

All quotes are from *A Course in Miracles*, copyright ©1992, 1999, 2007 by the Foundation for Inner Peace, 448 Ignacio Blvd., #306, Novato, CA 94949, www.acim.org and info@acim.org, and are used with permission.

Disclaimer: The information shared in this book is for educational and informational purposes only and is not intended to be viewed as medical or mental health advice. It is not designed to be a substitute for professional advice from your physician, therapist, attorney, accountant or any other health care practitioner or licensed professional. The Publisher and the Author do not make any guarantees as to the effectiveness of any of the techniques, suggestions, tips, ideas or strategies shared in this book as each situation differs. The Publisher and Author shall neither have liability nor responsibility with respect to any direct or indirect loss or damage caused or alleged by the information shared in this book related to your health, life or business or any other aspect of your situation. It's your responsibility to do your own due diligence and use your own judgment when applying any techniques or situations mentioned in or through this book. Any citations or sources of information from other organizations or websites are not endorsements of the information or content the website or organization provides or recommendations it may make. Please be aware that that any websites or references that were available during publication may not be available in the future.

"I want to understand the ALL of everything," I thought as a teenager. As an observer and artist in nature, my "all" mostly meant understanding life from the emotional and spiritual aspects of humanity. It took me two decades, reading a ton of books, studying, making observations, and feeling like something was missing, until I was introduced to a book that was said to be heavy, obscure and almost impossible to read. The warnings made me more curious and so I decided to open *A Course in Miracles Workbook (ACIM)*. It instantly made me feel like returning home—returning to Love. In all my years of yearning to understand life more deeply, *ACIM* finally offered me the depth and wisdom that I had longed to find.

When I started studying the *Workbook's* 365 daily lessons in the spring of 2014, I soon understood why it was considered so difficult: at times it was hard to stay awake, sometimes I battled with the wording and over-thinking, but one of the hardest struggles was to really inquire into how I defined God.

Fortunately for me, something miraculous started to happen when I kept trying to understand, fervently wrote my study notes, and showed up daily to dive deeper. After just a few days, a little angry (oh wow, was she grumpy back then!) stick figure girl popped out of my pen with clenched fists and a frown on her face. She winked at me and started to help me understand what I was reading.

One of my first doodle notes

With each lesson the tiny stick-figure, named Mira, took over more and more space on the pages of my notebook and as her heart started to open, so did mine. She filled my journey with hope, light and laughter! Whenever I took the *Course* too seriously, she hopped onto the page again, made me laugh out loud and relax.

Over the years, her messages have become lighter and lighter. No longer do I feel the need or urgency to "understand the ALL of everything". My time spent with *ACIM* has helped me figure out how to function in the world and find peace of mind.

The book in your hands is a collection of illustrations that illuminate a quote or an idea, or tell a story from each of the first 60 *ACIM Workbook* lessons. Overall, they represent a decade worth of shifts in perception that studying *ACIM* has brought me. If you want, you can follow the original lessons from the top of the pages or dive deeper with your own copy of *ACIM*.

It's all about walking home hand in hand with our sisters and brothers, following our heart, and letting miracles guide the way.

When studying something as complex as *A Course in Miracles*, doodling through it helps me grasp the ideas in a way that feels the most natural to me. I was ten years old when I first noticed that I learn through my hands—by drawing what I wanted to learn. Often, I feel that the learning happens when I ink or color the images I've drawn. Doodling is my meditation. It helps me to quiet my mind, connect with my heart, and hear what Love has to say.

For me, these first 60 lessons were the hardest lessons in the *Workbook*, because they shook up my thoughts and stirred my mind to help me loosen the ego's grip on it. The joy and light-heartedness that Mira sprinkled onto my notebook pages made studying feel less heavy. It lifted the thick veil of thought clouds, helped me move through them, and allowed more miracles to appear!

My hope is that this book may bring you many miracles like that too; that by illuminating this journey with illustrations, your studying may also feel easier and lighter. May this also ignite your curiosity to explore *A Course in Miracles* with wonder: where will it lead You?

Happy return to Love!

Elina Puohiniemi, 2024

Meet the Characters

MIRA is an ever-curious, joyful inner child. She shows us time and time again how choosing to follow our heart instead of listening to the ego brings us peace and happiness. She's our guide on this internal adventure—a journey within—that we are about to embark upon. Mira's message is HOPE and for you to

KEEP FOLLOWING YOUR HEART!

MIRA'S HEART represents her inner wisdom and the Love that she is (we all are!). In *ACIM* terms, the heart symbolizes the Holy Spirit, the mediator between the reality and illusions. Handing our problems over to the Holy Spirit connects us with Love—a Love that is all-encompassing and all-accepting.

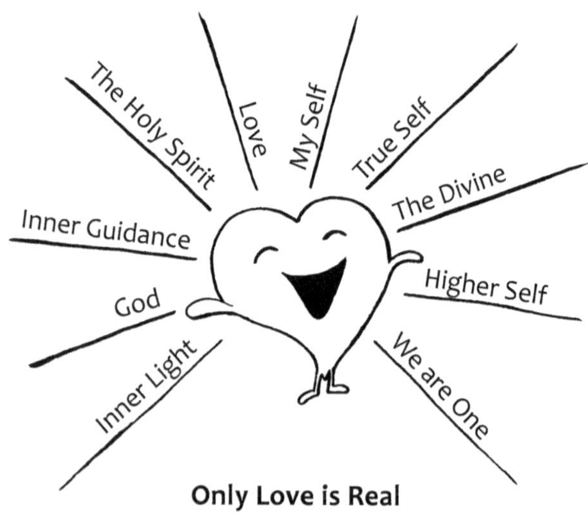

A LIZARD symbolizes the ego. It represents moments when we try to play it safe and make decisions from our primary brain (also called the lizard brain). It's all about survival. When we let the ego take the lead, fear rules our action and that's when defending, explaining and attacking occur. *A Course in Miracles* describes these moments as a call for Love. Choosing to let Love lead will undo the ego. It's good to remember that the ego always speaks first and loudest in its attempt to lead us away from Love.

MIRA'S FRIEND, SANDY, represents all the other people. She reflects Love and loyalty back to Mira or mirrors the ego, depending on which voice Mira chooses to listen to. With Sandy's help, Mira realizes that we can't learn these things alone:

When we forgive one another, we also forgive ourself.

Symbols Used in This Book

STARS symbolize miracles, which are shifts in perception according to *A Course in Miracles*. These shifts happen when we question the world that the ego shows us and start to wonder if there is another way of looking at the situation. Every time we feel lighter about any worry or concern that we have, and whenever we have any new insight to a struggle or situation we are facing, that's a miracle! Seeing reality as it is—as Love—is a miracle.

CLOUDS (aka **THOUGHT BUBBLES**) symbolize thoughts. When they are drawn as balloons on a string, the thoughts are being brought to our awareness. Grey and black clouds represent unloving/attack thoughts that take away our peace of mind in any way.

LIGHTNING BOLTS emphasize how much havoc our attack thoughts can create. It hurts! Other possible effects our thoughts could have are drawn as **RAIN-DROPS** and **HEARTS**.

THE GLOBE symbolizes the world, which can be observed with Love or through fear, depicting different results in each case.

SHINING LIGHT or **A CRACK IN THE CLOUDS** symbolizes the Truth or a revelation, which is a thought shared with Love—a real thought.

Also seen as "My Holiness" (pg. 64) symbolizing the Truth that is shone on us even when we are not aware or we resist.

A CLOTH symbolizes the act of forgiveness. With forgiveness, we can wipe away the blocks to Love's presence, move through them and discover that Love awaits on the other side.

All the symbols are drawn to help you move forward, towards more light and Love, and to bring you joy while studying *ACIM*.

**If the end goal is to be happy and joyful,
why not enjoy the journey too?**

Experiencing the Struggles with Love

Course in Miracles is often viewed as a very difficult read. It can repel potential readers during the first pages or make studying feel like a struggle later on. It is a course in changing the way we think—in undoing the ego—so the ego will put up a fight for sure. Here are some ways that I moved through the struggles with Love:

Reminded myself that all struggle comes from the ego and are a call for Love.

Whenever the language or wording of the *Course* made me anxious, I simplified the struggle by choosing words that resonated more with me. For example, I replaced "God" with "Love" quite freely. No harm done, because like the *Course* points out, putting too much emphasis on the words isn't necessary:

> "Words will mean little now. We use them but as guides
> on which we do not now depend. For now we seek direct
> experience of truth alone."
>
> W-pII.in.1:1-3

The same is true for masculine pronouns. My native language, Finnish, doesn't have gender pronouns, so it was easy to let Mira play with the ideas in her delightful girly way in the illustrations. She didn't mind if the quote above said "he/him/son/brother", because she knew that words are just the surface, and the Truth is that we are all One. We are all Love.

> "Stop terrorizing
> yourself with your
> thoughts!"
> Louise Hay

Instead, **ask for Love.**

"And love will come wherever it is asked."
W-pI.313.1:2

Just Accept

my first round of studying the lessons, my teacher, Marika Borg, gave me one simple piece of advice on how to study the *Course*:
"Just accept."

It became my guiding light and cure for overthinking. Every time I asked her a complex question, she patiently repeated:
"Just accept."

Her advice did the trick. It cleared my mind, made me smile, and helped me bounce me back to peace.

Everything that didn't bring me peace and joy just needed to be read and accepted—not immediately understood. In between the lines I read her advice as:
"Just trust the process, you're in good hands."

Now, all we need is a tiny sparkle of curiosity, an open mind,
a little willingness to keep going, and then
allow Love do the rest.

Start before you're ready.
Keep coming back to the lessons.
Just show up for Love.

This is the beginning of "undoing the way you see now."
W-pl.Intro.3:2

What I COULD see though, was that I needed to take the first step and commit to this journey.

1

This is hard!
It's freeing, but
also so sad!
I want to hold
onto the meanings
I've given things.
Giving up now is
NOT an option,
eh?
Just
trust the
process—
you're in
good
hands.

Remember to ask for help! Let your heart interpret your problems with Love.
Let me look at
that for you!
All is well!

The meaning I'd given everything I saw and experienced was in my mind. I no longer wanted to be stuck with what I'd imagined. I was curious to find out where Love would lead me.

I started wiping out all the old pathways of my think-ing—or at least made my best attempt to do so.

"The point of the exercises is to help you clear your mind of all past associations, to see things exactly as they appear to you now, and to realize how little you really understand about them."

W-pl.3.2:1

Now, having started to clear my mind, I wondered what my thoughts really were about then?

"The 'good' ones are but shadows of what lies beyond, and shadows make sight difficult."
W-pI.4.2:4

"The 'bad' ones are blocks to sight, and make seeing impossible."
W-pI.4.2:5

A staring contest with my unhappy thoughts was really exhausting because my thoughts never blinked first.

"I cannot keep this form of upset and
let the others go."
W-pl.5.6:3

6

I had been upset because I had thought it was THEM who had caused my upset, but actually it was my own thoughts that had blocked the sun and poured down on me.

Now, there was an added layer of beating myself up for it, too.
And how helpful was that?!

My tendency to define my future and present moment by my past experiences made moving forward really tricky.

Also, a thought rarely came alone. It usually was followed by quite a storm.

I understood that I shouldn't be doing this alone either.

"Ask for help,
Don't keep it all inside,
Let the Love in."
Robert Holden

Soon, the rain stopped and clouds parted.

What I saw was only my "thoughts projected outward."
W-pI.8.1:3

And the ego kept on bringing me more and more thoughts to keep me busy with my 'movies'.

I gave my thoughts a little loving shake to see if it would shake the whole picture. It did! In my experiment, I started giving a genuine smile—with a sparkle in my eyes—to people I didn't normally smile at. It instantly changed the movie in my mind about them! With this small gesture, I realized that our loving presence has great power!

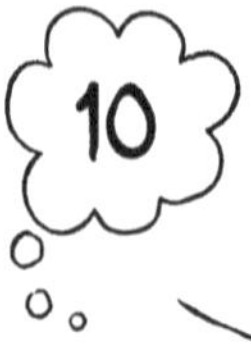

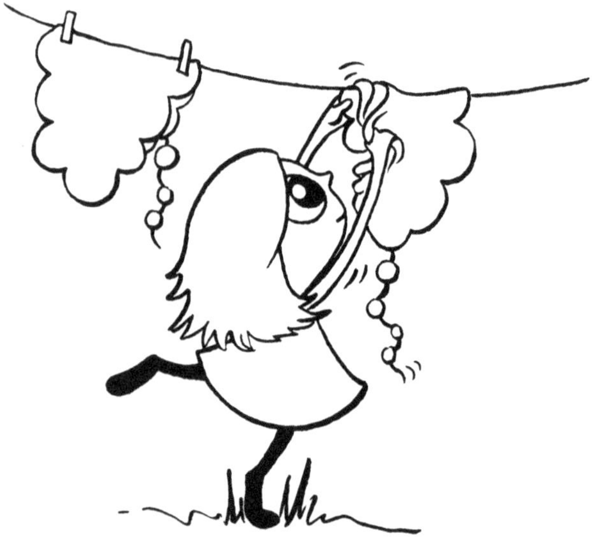

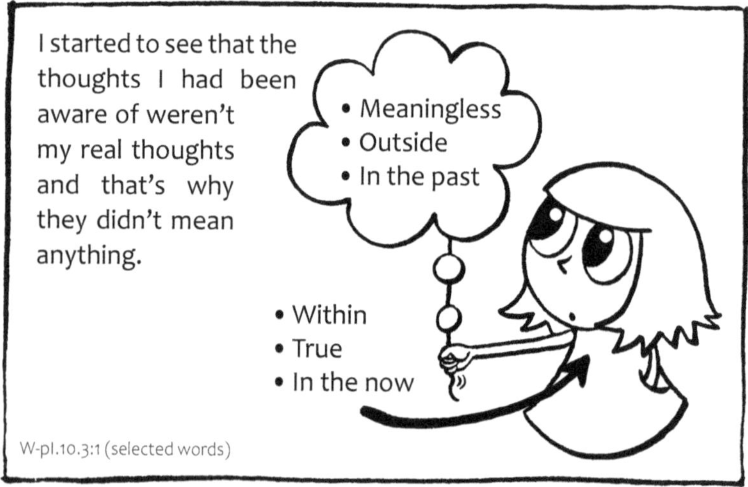

What if my thoughts were all blank and
their meaning was washed away?

I started to see that the thoughts I had been aware of weren't my real thoughts and that's why they didn't mean anything.

W-pI.10.3:1 (selected words)

"It seems as if the world determines
what you perceive."
W-pl.11.1:2

When the world just kept feeding me news of horrible events and accidents, making me increasingly upset and worried, I started wondering: What was going on?

It was because "... Your thoughts determine the world you see."
W-pl.11.1:3

Even if my thoughts were meaningless, and they showed me a meaningless world, it didn't stop me from trying to give it meaning.

Indeed, I had been busy giving meaning to everything and anything to hide its meaninglessness!

But the world is not "good" nor "bad". It just is.

Ah, imagine how peaceful life would be if all the labels fell off!

The labels started to drop the moment I became aware of the bigger picture of what was really going on.

It was time to decide whether I wanted to keep giving meaning to the world with the ego or if I could "accept the meaningless without fear" (W-pl.13.3:1) and let Love shine through the clouds like the sun.

"The world you see has nothing to do with reality. Some of [the horrors you see] are shared illusions, and others are part of your personal hell."

W-pI.14.1:4 & 6:3

This lesson gave me a headache the first time I studied it. It was so difficult to wrap my head around the concept of who created what? I was filled with many witty ideas to challenge the lesson's idea... Until I was once again reminded:

"Less thinking and more acceptance! JUST ACCEPT!"

Redefining God

Accepting doesn't come naturally to me, so I needed to pause and doodle some more to gain clarity on the concept of God at this point.

The idea of God as a judging, cruel, finger-pointing deity didn't feel right. Neither did it fit my ideal for a Creator to view God as an old man on a cloud who lets all the bad stuff happen in the world.

When I dug deeper, all I found was Love. To me, God is Love—the Love within us—the force of Life and energy, that connects us all at the core.

"You think you think them, and so you think you see them.
It is not seeing. It is image making."
W-pl.15.1:2 & 5-6

I'm an image-maker by profession and now my image-making skills were being asked to be replaced...

"Every thought you have contributes to truth or to illusion; either it extends the truth or it multiplies illusions . . . Every thought you have brings either peace or war; either love or fear."

W-pl.16.2:3 & 3:1

What if I sorted them out, I thought,
and only concentrated on
the happy, loving ones?

Dismissing my unhappy thoughts was a mistake.

I soon learned that unhappy thoughts were better teachers than happy ones for letting go and finding the Real thoughts. It was harder to see harm in happy thoughts, until I remembered that they are simply shadows of the Real Deal (see pg. 20). I saw how they could become a distraction too!

17

I painted the world with the color of my thoughts.

Tomorrow, I might not be—what a rollercoaster ride!

"It is always the thought that comes first, despite the temptation to believe that it is the other way around."

W-pI.17.1:3

What I saw in the news or through the eyes of my friend painted a picture of the world for me—if I allowed it.

If her way of seeing could affect how I perceive my world,
then my way of seeing could do the same for hers!

"I am not alone in
experiencing the
effects of my thoughts.
W-pI.19

"You want to be happy.
You want peace."
W-pI.20.2:4-5

"What you desire you will see."
W-pI.20.5:5

Angry? Me? No Way!

The first time I studied this lesson, I was in denial. It was impossible to find ". . . situations past, present or anticipated that arouse anger . . ." (W-pl.21.2:2) in me for the exercise. How could I see the situation differently, if I didn't even see it? I could identify many other emotions, but not anger. I had hidden it well.

Five years later, I had to admit there might have been anger in my past—still not in the present though!

Since then, I've learned to identify anger in the present moment, too. But oh wow, it can be tricky. It's so easily masked, veiled or suppressed in some way.

Now, I no longer want to shove my unloving thoughts aside because they'd take away my peace of mind. I'm determined to let Love lead, let anger come and go, and see the situations differently!

My determination to stay on the path of Love helps me to vigilantly catch all the unloving thoughts—tiny ones, too.

Holding on to a bunch of attack thoughts in reserve—expecting others to attack—definitely takes away my peace of mind!

The ego might think it's smart to be prepared like that, but is it really?

"There is no point in trying to change the world. It is incapable of change because it is merely an effect."

W-pI.23.2:3-4

W-pI.23.5:2 (selected words)

"But there is indeed a point in changing your thoughts about the world. Here you are changing the cause. The effect will change automatically."

W-pI.23.2:5-7

In my search for happiness, I've often taken detours, convinced I would find happiness where it wasn't.

W-pI.24.6:2 (selected words)

Off I was again, steering away from the Path of Love, where I would have met Joy, Peace and Happiness.

Let Miracles Guide You Back!

"This world is full of miracles. They stand in shining silence next to every dream of pain and suffering, of sin and guilt."

T-28.II.12:1-2

It became very clear to me that I no longer wanted to make plans and set goals with the ego anymore.

Letting go of the need to identify with the ego helped me stick to the present moment and experience life in the here and now— not in my dreams about the future.

"Nothing except your thoughts can attack you."
W-pI.26.4:2

My attack thoughts always came back like a boomerang and hurt me—no matter how justified I thought they'd been.

If my attack thoughts hurt me so much, how would I be without them?

I made a list of all things light, joyful, and peaceful. Then, I made another list where I dove deeper into each of them with more detail. I spent some happy moments thinking how they would realize in my life.

I'd be blissful: bubbling, sparkling bliss would surface from deep within. I'd feel free—free to be me. I'd smile more. I'd feel I am, do, and have enough. I'd be relaxed, confident... and the list went on.

How about you: How would you be without your attack thoughts?

What if we trusted that what Love will
show us is something so much better
than what we could ever imagine?

*Vision = Seeing through the eyes of Love

What would it feel like to look at everything with the same awe and loving curiosity that a child would: ". . . asking what it is, rather than telling it what it is." (W-pI.28.3:3)

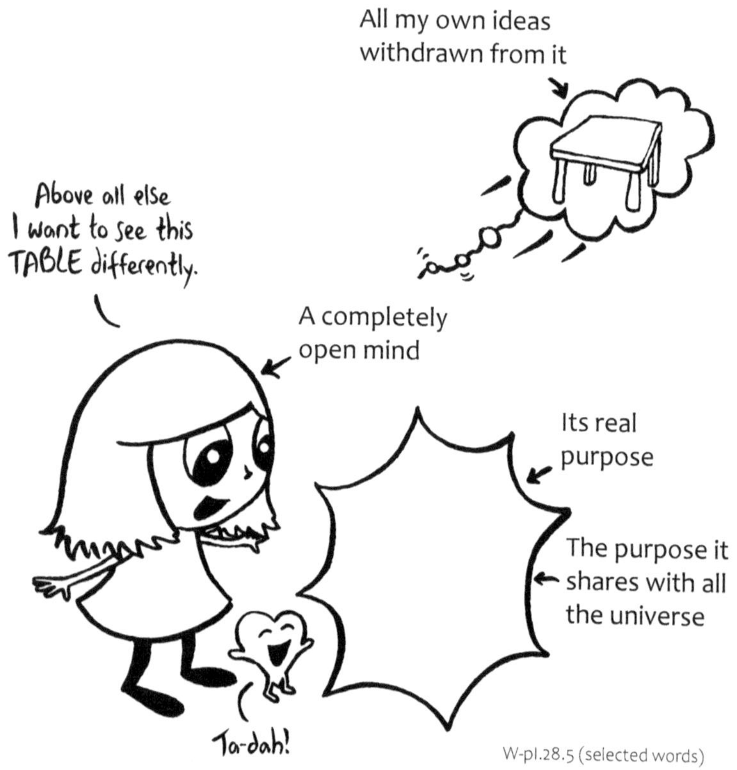

W-pI.28.5 (selected words)

I experimented with this in parenting, relationships, and my encounters with others. I tried to ask, rather than tell, and stay curious and open: Who are they? Where are they on their journey? I tried to keep my own assumptions, expectations, limiting beliefs, and thoughts about them at bay. It was freeing!

"... Look on all things with love, appreciation and open-mindedness."

W-pI.29.3:1

To always see the world, my relationships, life around me—and in the news—with the eyes of Love... wouldn't that be something?

30 GOD IS IN EVERYTHING I SEE BECAUSE GOD IS IN MY MIND.

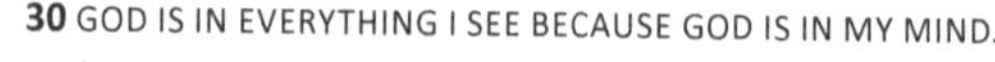

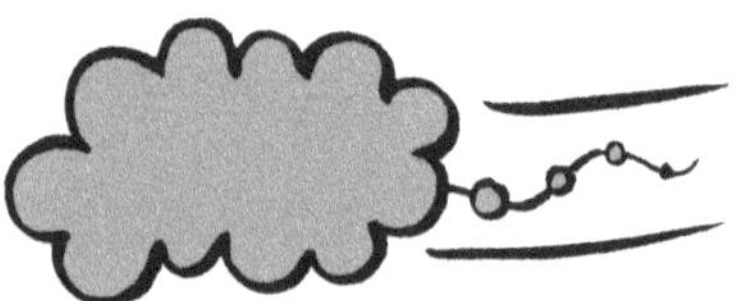

"... We are trying to join with what we see, rather than keeping it apart from us."

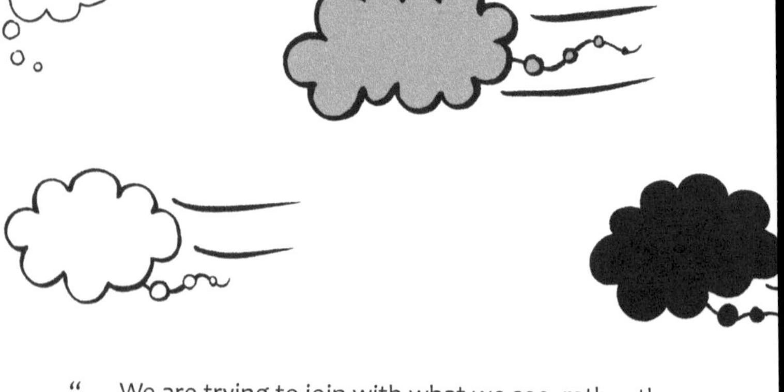

W-pI.30.2:4

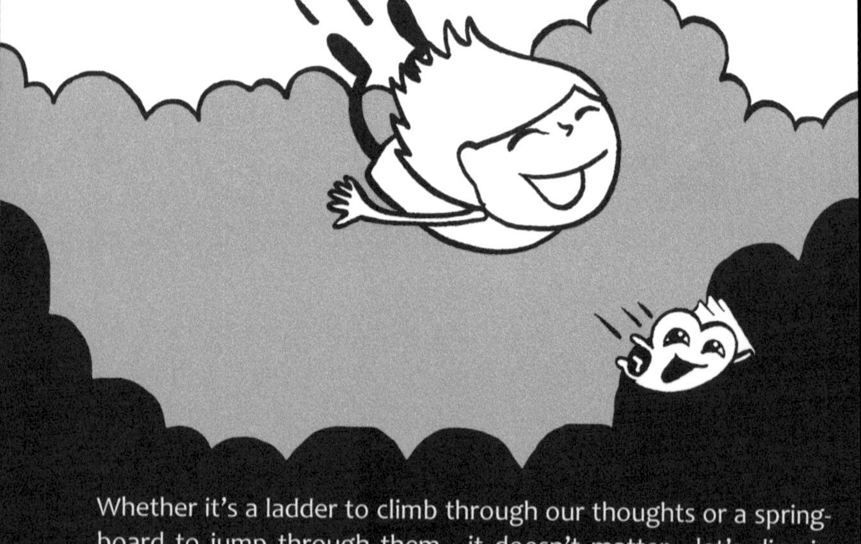

Whether it's a ladder to climb through our thoughts or a springboard to jump through them—it doesn't matter—let's dive in courageously! Meeting our thoughts with Love, acceptance, and willingness to let go is all that counts!

31

". . . You are making a declaration of independence in the name of your own freedom. And in your freedom lies the freedom of the world."

W-pI.31.4:2-3

"You can give [the world you invented] up as easily as you made it up."

W-pI.32.1:2-3

I had the power to choose and change my life. I was not a victim. There was ALWAYS another way to see.

"While you want it you will see it; when you no longer want it, it will not be there for you to see."

W-pI.32.1:5

There was always more of my own stuff to heal first. I soon noticed that all my attempts to give advice and fix things for others didn't only make them put up their defenses, but it was also a distraction for me from taking responsibility and healing myself first.

I realized—even if it was hard for a fixer-upper like me—that it was better to just BE there for her and keep looking for Love within.

There must be another way of looking at this...

What if, until now, I'd tried to do it all upside-down and that's why it felt so hard?

When I looked at the situation differently, I could find Love. It was right there—everywhere! My life turned right side up. Just like that!

34

"Peace of mind is clearly an internal matter. It must begin with your own thoughts, and then extend outward."
W-pI.34.1:2-3

My happy thoughts of peace had all just been waiting to be noticed. In any situation, we can simply invite them to appear. Look, there they are!

It was through the cracks in layers of ego that
my inner light started to shine through.

But on some days, I resisted the whole idea of being holy, and this is what happened: Meet Grumpy-Mira!

When my holiness didn't shine from within, these tiny sparks of HOPE kept showing up. They could be something like a compliment or a smile. I started wondering if there was some truth to being holy after all and gave the idea a chance.

What signs of YOUR holiness have you spotted lately?

36

Little by little, the light I had only spotted outside of me started shining bright from within.

Eventually, the light shone on everything around me, too!

"Your purpose is to see the world through your holiness.

Thus are you and the world blessed together."

W-pl.37.1:2-3

"Your holiness . . . can remove all pain, can end all sorrow, and can solve all problems."

W-pI.38.2:4

Now, in an ideal scenario I wouldn't have had any reason to keep dismissing my unloving thoughts after this lesson. I'd have called them all out and blessed them by bringing them into my light, but if only the spiritual path was that straightforward!
For a long while, I was stuck wondering how on earth I could BLESS my unloving thoughts—I had plenty of reasons not to.

"It's imperative for your own salvation that you see
[your unloving thoughts] differently."

W-pI.39.7:1-2

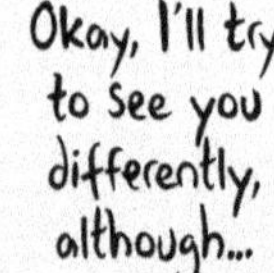
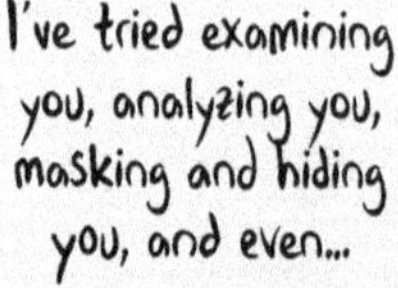

Then I figured that I hadn't yet tried to see my unloving thoughts through my holiness. I gave it a try.

"I am happy, peaceful, loving and contented.
I am calm, quiet, assured and confident."
W-pI.40.3:5, 8

For more attributes, return to your answers on the question "How would I be without my attack thoughts?" on page 51.

"Deep within you is everything that is perfect, ready
to radiate through you and out into the world."

W-pI.41.3:1

"It is His strength, not your own, that gives you power.
It is His gift, not your own, that offers vision to you."

W-pI.42.1:4-5

Love quietly whispered all the secrets of the world to me.

At anytime that we struggle to hear these whispers, we can hand our problems over to the Holy Spirit, the mediator between perception and knowledge.

Internal
Oneness
God
Love
Healed perception
Knowledge

In the company of the ego, we feel more and more separated from each other and God/Love feels distant and very much external. Like something that isn't for us. The more we pause, breathe, and open up to listen to the tiny whispers from our inner guide, the lighter life becomes.

Forgiveness brings us closer and closer to feeling oneness until finally the light shines from within us. Love becomes internalized.

When I let the light shine from within me, it emptied the ego's attempts to sell me shiny objects—in my light they lost their glory.

No matter how hard the ego tried, it could never offer gifts such as Love. Love's gifts bring miracles and multiply when shared.

"My real thoughts are in my mind.
I would like to find them."
W-pI.45.6:4-5

46

Bouncing Back to Love Through Forgiveness

Sometimes it has felt impossible to turn things around with my so called "enemies"—even with my best friend.

Until I remembered that all the ego behavior was a call for Love!

With forgiveness, I released myself from illusions: my enemies
became my saviors.

"Fear condemns and Love forgives."
W-pI.46.2:2

"It's only a thought and
a thought can be changed."
Louise Hay

"It is not by trusting yourself that you
will gain confidence. But the strength of
God in you is successful in all things."

W-pI.47.5:3-4

"The awareness that there is nothing to fear shows that somewhere in your mind, though not necessarily in a place you recognize as yet, you have remembered God, and let His strength take the place of your weakness. The instant you are willing to do this there is indeed nothing to fear."

W-pI.48.3:2-3

I'm Safe, or am I?

Wouldn't it be better to say "I'm safe" than "there's nothing to fear" I wondered at this point, because sometimes even mentioning the word "fear" instantly made my fears surface.

But no, the process of letting go of illusions means not being afraid of ANY of them!

Let's start by acknowledging our illusions and fears—and reminding ourselves that they are not ALL there is. Then let's keep reading the small print (which the ego always adds to every thought) and forgive ourselves for believing in our illusions and trusting in our own strength. Let's give ourselves grace and lean more on Love!

W-pI.49.1-2 (selected words)

No matter how loudly the ego yells or how hard it tries to pull us off the Path of Love for another detour, we can always pause, ask for help, and connect with the Truth—anytime!

"[The Love of God] will lift you out of every trial, and raise you high above all the perceived dangers of this world into a climate of perfect peace and safety."

W-pI.50.3:1-2

In the end life is simple—and Love is even simpler; we already have EVERYTHING within us that we need. Except that...

...it doesn't always appear to be so!
This staying aware and awake is something we need to be reminded of again and again in each moment and with every decision we make. To make it easier to remember, let's review the journey so far with more images. Let's bask in all the Love that there is!

Where there's no Love, there's judgment.

I've singled out her attacks one by one for investigation.

I've kept analyzing what she said or did a day, a year, two decades ago—digging deeper and deeper in search of meaning.

In my attempt to understand the ALL of everything, all I found was more questions, and got more lost.

Soon, I realized that I had taken a detour with the ego—again.

I asked myself: Do I want to keep struggling or be happy instead? Am I willing to "make room for what can be seen and understood and loved"?

(W-pI.51.3:6)

I was willing to let go of my old thought system and commit to keeping only what I'd think with Love.

"Reality is never frightening.
Reality brings only perfect
peace."
W-pI.52.1:2, 4

"When I have
forgiven myself
and remembered
Who I am, I will
bless everyone and
everything I see."
W-pI.52.2:5

"Let me learn to give the
past away, realizing that
in so doing I am giving
up nothing."
W-pI.52.3:6

"The choice is not whether to see
the past or the present; the choice is
merely whether to see or not."

W-pI.52.4:4

53

"Reality is not insane, and I have real thoughts as well as insane ones. I can therefore see a real world, if I look to my real thoughts as my guide for seeing."

W-pl.53.1:4-5

"I am grateful that this world is not real,
and that I need not see it at all
unless I choose to value it."

W-pl.53.2:6

"Let me remember the power of my decision, and recognize where I really abide."
W-pI.53.4:6

"... My real thoughts ... cast their beneficent light on what I see."
W-pI.53.5:4

It's okay that it takes time and patience to unlearn fear-based thinking. Let's take it one day, one step, one thought at a time and enjoy the journey as much as we can!

"I'm alone in nothing. Everything I think or say or do teaches all the universe."

W-pI.54.4:2-3

My real thoughts help others move through
their own thought clouds.

55
Here's some more!
That was so fun, I'll definitely choose more of that!
There's more where that came from.
Follow me!

No Matter What...

We all have the ability to share Love, spread miracles, and enjoy the journey—no matter what!

Despite the fact that I'd given my peace of mind away in an attempt to make peace with the world…

… Love had waited patiently by my side to be noticed.

Temporarily forgetting that I am Love (due to detours with the ego) never means that I've lost Love.

"Behind every image I have made, the truth remains unchanged."
W-pI.56.4:2

"My chains are loosened. I can drop them off merely by desiring to do so."

W-pI.57.1:3-4

"I made up the prison in which I see myself. All I need do is recognize this and I am free."

W-pI.57.2:2-3

"When I see the world as a place of freedom, I realize that it reflects the laws of God instead of the rules I made up for it to obey."

W-pI.57.4:2

And really, when did the world ever obey my rules?

"As I share the peace of the world with my brothers, I begin to understand that this peace comes from deep within myself. I begin to understand the holiness of all living things, including myself, and their oneness with me."

W-pI.57.5:3, 5:6

58
I can see LOVE everywhere—even in the mirror!
What a joy it is to share this with you! 
My inner light shines away all illusions!

I am at peace.

What would you have me do?
Follow me!

59 A Journey from Your Head to Your Heart

See, there's a crack through which the light shines!

So light!
This is what our shared thought looks and feels like!

"What could there be to fear in a world that
I have forgiven, and that has forgiven me?"

W-pI.60.3:6

"There is not a moment in which His
Voice fails to direct my thoughts,

guide my actions and lead my feet."
W-pI.60.4:3

Are you ready to
open your eyes?

"As I open my eyes, His Love lights
up the world for me to see."
W-pI.60.5:3

Oops, but here we go again! No matter our best intentions to stay on the Path of Love, these detours with the ego sometimes happen. It's okay!

"Learning is in the returning."
Hollie Holden

It can take some time before we remember to pause and recognize what happened, but eventually we rise again, through the clouds, and reach for the miraculously starry skies.

On the following pages, you will find three useful reminders from this journey for a rainy day and three things worth knowing about miracles that help us stay on the path for a little longer each time. Will you listen to the ego or follow your heart?

Ask Love for a Second Opinion,
I have a problem...
Can you take a look at this?
Choose Freely,
I choose Love!

And Remember to Laugh!

Whenever the ego tries to hold you back from the Truth—from Love—remember that you don't need to take it so seriously.

"You can indeed afford to laugh at fear thoughts,
remembering that God goes with you wherever you go."
W-pI.41.10:1

A Tiny Miracle Guide

"But," you might wonder, "what about those miracles?"

Even though, the first 60 lessons of the *Workbook* don't yet offer much information on miracles, each lesson can bring us one or many!

When we let go of the fearful thinking with the ego—and let Love in—miracles occur naturally.

"A miracle is a shift in perception from fear to Love."
Marianne Williamson

120

Every expression of Love clears the way for new, joyful and lighter thoughts— and thus bring miracles to us!

What is your favorite way to express Love?
Is it through art and creativity, smile and connection, food and care-taking, sharing deep wisdom, or maybe just by being you?

Keep shining your light and share any miracles you've got!

We're never far from our next miracle!

It's right there waiting to appear.

The shortest way to meet your next miracle is through the thoughts that block the presence of Love.

Wipe them clean with forgiveness, go through the clouds, and return to Love!

"Your next miracle is only ever a thought away."
Elloa Atkinson

And off they went and shared
their miracles with the world.

Acknowledgments

Although I started my *A Course in Miracles* journey by myself, I wasn't alone for long. I couldn't have gone through the lessons without my teachers and study buddies. My deepest gratitude goes to my teachers Marika Borg, Hollie and Robert Holden, and the Holden's online study group, *Everyday Miracles*. Special thanks to Brigitte, Louise, and Hannah for our wonderful conversations on these topics.

Creating this book would have been impossible without help and therefore I'm deeply grateful for Kathleen Anderson de Miranda, Lisa Carter, and Jessica Tudos for their support and help with finding the right words. A huge thanks goes to my test readers Vaylu, Lynda, Adina, Sue, and my parents, who gave me insightful feedback when I didn't know how to move forward. I'm grateful to my brother Timotito for sharing this artistic lifetime and this book journey with me. And big thanks to all my patrons on Patreon for being there through the ups and downs of my book journeys.

My greatest heartfelt gratitude goes to my sons who spent their childhood witnessing me go through the study and creative journeys with *ACIM* and Mira. Finding their drawings of grumpy Mira scribbled on my desktop and then later hearing them read my books out loud has been such joy! Last but not least, thank you, Teemu, for all your Love. It has lit up my life and kept me grounded through all the storms that I've created in my mind.

About the Author & Illustrator

Elina Puohiniemi, aka elinap, is an author, illustrator, and the creator of the Mira(cle)Doodles series. She lives in Finland with her husband, two teenage sons, and their poodle.

Raised without religion, but naturally spiritual, Elina has always been curious about old wisdom traditions and different religions. In 2010, she started to illustrate her spiritual path and insights. Her first character was a lizard that helped her see the past with more clarity. The next character was Elwira, with whom elinap illustrated spiritual insights for a famous Finnish wellness website on a monthly basis for several years.

But Elina struggled with illustrating Elwira. Later, she described it feeling like her hand had been in a knot. Having drawn all her life—through an art school and commissioned book illustrations—the familiar connection with an idea and her pen dancing on paper wasn't there—it had disappeared! Fortunately, miracles started to occur when her path led her forward, through life coaching and Master Coach studies which led her toward *A Course in Miracles*.

She was surprised by the birth of her doodle character, Mira, and a renewed joy and effortlessness in drawing that accompanied Mira's arrival. With Mira it wasn't so serious. Being a stick-figure, Mira conveyed ideas without pressure to be perfect. Mira's ever-changing and always-evolving appearance also brought elinap personal messages that helped her open her knotted hand and free her from the previous illustrating struggles.

Now, ten years and thousands of Mira(cle)Doodles later, Mira keeps evolving. She's now coming to life as a wooden puppet through elinap's own creative hands.

Doodling Miracles
- Inspiring Joy & Reflection –

Mira(cle)Doodles are illustrations from a spiritual path, born from a need to question the ego's ways and to follow the heart no matter what comes along. They simplify and explain life's struggles and spiritual challenges with a loving twist and show how it's possible to choose Love and be at peace in any moment.

Originating from doodles drawn on the pages of a notebook, Mira(cle)Doodles bring out an authentic glimpse of a spiritual journey. In their delightful illumination of inner musings, they help us to connect with our own inner wisdom and deepen our understanding of life and Love.

Try It Out Yourself
If you also enjoy writing notes and journaling while you study, try and see if your own little stick figure person pops out of your pen one day to help you decipher what you want to learn—adding even more joy in your journey!

Whenever you feel stuck, just ask:
"WHAT WOULD LOVE DO?"
And listen to your heart answer on the pages of your notebook.

> "Mira" in Latin means "wonder", in Spanish it's "look", in Russian "mir" stands for "peace", and in Japanese "mirai" is "future". "Clé" in French means "a key".
> Together, they are "a miracle"!
> That makes Mira(cle)Doodles keys for looking at a peaceful future with wonder. (The future starting with the next thought we'll have.)

And This Is How Mira(cle)Doodles Are Born!

Other Titles by Cling

MIRA 2
Astonishing Moments & Turning Points (2023)

MIRA
Glimpses of Life & Whispers from the Heart (2022)

THE FOUR PHASES OF CREATIVITY
A Path to Unleashing the Natural Flow of Your Creativity (2021)

COLOR YOUR DREAMS TRUE & LEARN TO TRUST THE PROCESS
10 Simple Coloring Exercises to Help You Magnetize Your Dreams
and Enjoy the Journey (2016)

More Mira(cle)Doodles at
www.doodlingmiracles.com